Repentance

An examination of the doctrine of repentance from a scriptural perspective.

by Michael Pearl

D1316522

Repentance®
Copyright © 2000 by Michael and Debi Pearl
ISBN-13: 978-1-892112-09-4
ISBN-10: 1-892112-09-4
First printing: 1992
Second printing: 2000
Third printing: 2007

Visit www.NoGreaterJoy.org for information on other products
produced by No Greater Joy Ministries.

Requests for information should be addressed to:
No Greater Joy Ministries Inc.
1000 Pearl Road, Pleasantville, TN 37033 USA

All scripture quotations are taken from the King James Holy Bible.

Cover: Danny Bulanadi, Clint Cearly and Aaron Aprile
Interior layout by Lynne Hopwood

Printed in the United States of America

Table of Contents

Introduction

It is most commonly thought that repentance is a separate work of God that must precede faith—the first rung on a ladder to God. The fundamental question is, "When the Bible warns the sinner to repent or perish, what is the nature of that repentance?" When a gospel tract or an evangelist tells a sinner that he must "repent of his sins" in order to be saved, precisely what is he requiring? We agree that it is a critical issue. To fail to do what God requires would result in eternal damnation. There are many believers worried about their repentance. They wonder if they "did it right." I am convinced that some did and some didn't. This work is designed to put hearts to rest in Christ and to correct error.

The Bible uses the word *repent* in more than one way. Ignorance of this fact has led to debate, with each side presenting Scriptural evidence in contradiction to the other. As long as you think that there is a single definition for repentance, you will arrive at conclusions in some instances. When you understand the various ways that the Bible uses the word *repent*, you can then accurately understand its meaning as it applies to the gospel of Christ.

Ultimately, our purpose is to answer the simple question, "What must I do to be saved?" What part does repentance play, and exactly what is it? Is it something that the sinner must do or something that God does for him? Is it possible to believe and not repent? Is it possible to repent and not follow through with faith?

I invite you to follow me in an examination of all 112 uses of the word *repent* as found in the King James Bible.

Overview

God's thoughts on repentance (or any subject) are contained in words found in sentences, paragraphs, chapters, individual books, and ultimately in the combination of all 66 books of the Bible. To understand a doctrine as God intended we must first understand the individual words of each sentence that addresses the subject. For that reason, sound Bible study begins with a careful examination of word meanings. We do not rely upon Greek, Hebrew, or English dictionaries. We do not sell ourselves short by relying on the commentaries of other men. The Bible comes with its own built-in dictionary. It is there that we go to obtain accurate definitions. This little book is about an accurate definition of one word—repent.

This work is as much an example of how to study your Bible as it is a study on the word *repent*. It is documentation of the process by which I arrived at my conclusions. You will be able to examine all my reasoning on every verse. For that reason, this will be the most transparent study you have ever read.

To begin the process of defining the word, I made a complete list of every usage of the word *repent* in all its forms—repent, repentance, repented, repenting, repenteth. It is found 112 times in the KJV. Strong's Concordance omits one reference, and the computer programs are impossible. Several writers gave different counts. It took several hours to get an accurate count.

For the purpose of examination, I then broke all the references down and listed them according to common characteristics. For the sake of counting, we do not differentiate between the different tenses or the noun or verb usage. While cross-checking the various categories for redundancies or omissions, I was suddenly struck with an amazing numerical pattern.

Repent is used 39 times in reference to God's repentance or the lack of it. There are 39 books in the Old Testament.

Repent is used 66 times in reference to man's repentance regarding sin or God. There are 66 books in the Bible. Of the 66 uses, repent is used 6 times in groups of 6. Six is the number of man in Scripture.

3

It is used:

- 6 times in reference to man's repentance regarding sin or God.
- 6 times John the Baptist preached repentance.
- 6 times repentance and baptism are mentioned together.
- 6 times the Apostles (excluding Paul) preached repentance.
- 6 times in the book of Revelation we are told that the heathen will not repent.
- 6 times in the book of Revelation the Church is called to repent.

Repent is used seven times regarding something non-religious –man-to-man repentance. Seven is the number of completion. In these seven references is found a complete illustration of the natural definition of repentance.

Repent is used 39 times pertaining to God repenting or not repenting. There are 39 books in the Old Testament. God repents only in the Old Testament, never in the New.

Repent is used seven times in reference to God's repentance regarding sending judgment on a people for their sin. If they will repent, He will repent. As the judgments of God during the tribulation come in sevens, so it is here.

Repent is used seven times telling us that God has determined not to repent in regard to His judgments. Again, this is consistent with the number seven in regard to complete judgment.

Of course, you won't find these amazing numbers in just any book with the word "Bible" printed on it. It is only in the Lion itself – The Authorized, King James Bible. In it God has embellished His Word with unessential, yet delightful confirmations of His ongoing preservation of the words of Scripture in the English language. A study of repentance is an example of His exactness in delivering the Word. Pure doctrine, as a jewel set on a relief of mathematical improbabilities, assures us of His attention to even the least detail. If God has so carefully packaged His truths, our diligence in searching them out should be no less thorough.

Man-to-Man Repentance (7 uses)

Man repents before man in matters that are earthly, carnal, non-religious, or secular. These seven, non-doctrinal passages will give us a very good understanding of the nature of repentance itself, before we get into doctrinal passages that provoke greater emotion.

1. In *Ex. 13:17.* God led the Jews by a route that would prevent them from possibly engaging in warfare, *"Lest peradventure the people repent when they see war, and they return to Egypt."*

They were in danger of repenting of having left Egypt, of reversing their exodus and returning the way they had come.

2. & 3. *Judg. 21:6.* The children of Israel, due to a conflict with the tribe of Benjamin, swore to not give their daughters in marriage to the Benjaminites. In a terrible battle, the men of Benjamin had been reduced to only 600, with none of their females left alive. Because of the oath of the other tribes, the tribe of Benjamin was in peril of either extinction or adulteration of their seed—which would occur if they married outside their ethnic group. *Judg. 21:6 "And the children of Israel repented them for Benjamin their brother, and said, there is one tribe cut off from Israel this day."* Verse 15 uses the word *repented* also. This repentance was a change of mind and **action** that ultimately provided daughters of Israel to the 600 men of Benjamin.

4. *Matt. 21:28, 29,* *"But what think ye? A certain man had two sons; he came to the first, and said, Son go work today in my vineyard. He answered and said, I will not: but afterwards he repented, and went."*

This non-religious, common, everyday usage of the word throws much light on a simple definition. To do what he previously would not do was to repent.

5. & 6. *2 Cor. 7:8,* *"For though I made you sorry with a letter, I do not repent, though I did repent...."*

The letter of 2 Corinthians was a hard rebuke to the Corinthians. When Paul first saw how much sorrow it caused, he changed his mind about having written it. But, when he later saw the fruit of their repentance, he unrepented. He repented of his having repented. He took back the thought that he had made a mistake in writing as he had. He changed his mind about having changed his mind. Any genuine change of mind is repentance, in regard to the intentions.

7. Heb. 12:17. Esau, despising his birthright, sold it to his younger brother for a bowl of stew. *"...afterward, when he would have inherited the blessing, he was rejected; for he found no place of repentance, though he sought it carefully with tears."* When it came time to receive his inheritance, Esau saw his mistake. Plead, beg, or weep, Jacob could not be moved.

Notice what repentance is not: It is not a mere desire to change. It is not sorrow, regret, or tears. Repentance is not a state of mind or heart. It is not subjective, not an intention. Repentance, in this case, would have been to get back his blessing and birthright. He couldn't, so it is said, *"...he found no place of repentance."*

Conclusion to Man-to-Man Repentance

Repentance is, first, a secular word describing a complete turn-around on any stated issue. The context defines the nature of repentance in any particular usage. One could repent of going to the grocery store, or of visiting the relatives in the summer. One must first define the issue and its counterpart before the nature of repentance in that particular case can be understood.

God's Repentance (39 uses)

Introduction

That's right. God repents. The reason that this is so shocking to many is because of the common misunderstanding of repentance. As we examine all 39 uses of *repent* in reference to God's repentance or the stated lack thereof, our main purpose is to establish Biblical definitions. The Scripture should purge us of error and give us an accurate understanding of an otherwise most misused word.

God Repents From His Own Actions

Gen. 6:6, "...it repented the Lord that he had made man on the earth."

6

God's repentance reversed his actions. He who originally chose to place man on the earth now acts to destroy him. Grace allowed eight exceptions out of millions.

I Sam. **15:11,** *"It repented me that I have set up Saul to be king...."*

1 Sam. **15:35,** *"...and the Lord repented that he had made Saul king...."*

God's repentance was more than sorrow or a change of mind. He immediately anoints David to be king in Saul's stead. Saul dies in battle.

Observation
Repentance is a complete reversal of the issue, not just a desire for reversal. Since God does not do wrong, yet God repents, we can conclude that repentance is not necessarily a turn from wrong doing to right doing, unless, of course, the context defines it as such.

God Is Asked to Repent

Ex. 32:12, 14; Ps. 90:13; Jonah 3:9.

Ex. **32:12,** *"Turn from thy fierce wrath, and repent of this evil against thy people."*

Moses actually **commands God** to repent, not on the basis of moral rightness, but on the basis of His covenant with Abraham.

Ex. **32:14,** *"...And the Lord repented of the evil which he thought to do unto his people."*

This interchange of flesh with Deity is amazing. It seems to be a role reversal. God is about to justly destroy the entire seed of Abraham, which He had just delivered from Egyptian bondage. Their repeated sin has provoked Him to wrath, but Moses' reminder of God's covenant with Abraham moves God to repentance.

Observation
Since sinful man can call upon the Holy God to repent, it is obvious that repentance can be something other than the act of turning from sin.

God Repents from Sending Evil
("evil" as in physical calamity, war, disease, etc.)

Jer. 26:19; 42:10; Ex. 32:14; Judg. 2:18; 2 Sam. 24:16;
1 Chr. 21:15; Amos 73:6; Jonah 3:10, 4:2; Ps. 106:45.

Ex. 32:14, *"...And the Lord repented of the evil which he thought to do unto his people."*

Out of love of righteousness, God chastens His people. This chastisement is called *evil*. He allows a space for man to repent *(Rev. 2:21)*. If man does not turn from his sin, then God will not turn from His judgment. His judgment could ultimately lead to death.

In the passages listed above, God repents (lifting His judgment) when He determines that it is wise to do so. He does not always wait for men to repent. He may also lift His chastisement, being moved by their suffering, even though they do not turn from their disobedience. *(Judg. 2:18; 2 Sam. 24:16; 1 Chron. 21:15; Amos 7:3-6)*. Or He is moved by His covenant *(Ex. 32:14; Ps. 106:45)*.

Observation

That God repents of sending evil judgments does not imply that He was wrong to judge thus in the first place. As earthly circumstances change, so do God's methods. As God deals with the "infirmity of the flesh," his course of action is altered according to the need to fulfill his desired end.

Since God repents, repentance is not doing penance. Any change of relationship or method of dealing can be called repentance. Moral status is not implied either—only the act of turning. By way of definition, we see that it is a total reversal in regard to the stated issue.

God's Future Repentance in Sending Evil or Judgment

Jer. 18:8; 26:3, 13; Joel 2:13, 14; Ps. 135:14; Deut. 32:36.

Jer. 18:8, *"If that nation, against whom I have pronounced, turn from their evil, I will repent of the evil that I thought to do unto them."*

In this verse, God's repenting from his evil designs of judgment are conditioned upon the nation repenting from moral evil.

God had real plans to destroy them, and when He changed His mind it was called repentance.

Observation
Repentance may involve only the intentions, if that is the subject, as it was in this case.

Spiritual Lesson
If you are in the grip of God's chastisement—repent—turn from your sins and do them no more. Then He will repent of chastening you. Compare *Heb. 12:6-11* with *James 5:14-16.*

God Repents of Doing Good

Jer. 18:10, "If it do evil in my sight (nation), that it obey not my voice, then I will repent of the good, wherein I said I would benefit them."

Observation
By itself, the word *repent* means to turn in the opposite direction. There is no moral or immoral implication in the word itself. There is no religion, faith, or sorrow implied. Only the context gives direction and nature to the use of the word. Repent from what? Repent to what? In this case, God repents of doing good. His former direction was to bless them—do them good, but if they respond incorrectly, God warns that He will reverse his policy of blessing to a policy of cursing—in which case He would be repenting.

God Determines Not to Repent

Ps. 110:4; Jer. 4:28; Ezk. 24:14; Heb. 7:21; Hos. 13:14; Rom. 11:29; 1 Sam. 15:29.
Study carefully these seven uses of the word wherein God will not repent.

1. *1 Sam. 15:29.* God repented of making Saul king and announced his demise. God says of His decision to pull Saul from the throne that He will not repent. There was no condition under which God would reverse His decision to dethrone Saul. God would not repent of His repentance. In other words, God would not turn from His turning.

2. Ezek. 24:14. God determines to send the *"bloody city,"* Jerusalem, into Babylonian captivity. It was too late to reverse His decision. Neither their extreme suffering nor His covenant would turn Him.

3. & 4. Ps. 110:4; Heb. 7:21, *"The Lord sware and will not repent, thou art a priest forever after the order of Melchisedec...."*
God has put Himself under oath to eternally retain Christ as a high priest for His children. Nothing in man's failures could ever cause God to go back on this.

5. Jer. 4:28. This apparently speaks of the Great Tribulation. God has prophesied Jacob's Trouble, a time of *"great tribulation, such as was not since the beginning of the world to this time, no, nor ever shall be" (Matt. 24:21).* It will come, and neither the "Man of Peace" nor the "Dragon" himself can stop it. God will not repent.

6. Hos. 13:14, God will not repent in His commitment to redeem Ephraim (Israel) from their dispersion and judgment.

7. Rom. 11:25 29, *"...blindness in part is happened to Israel, until...all Israel shall be saved...this is my covenant... they are beloved for the Father's sake...for the gifts and calling of God are without repentance."*
Clearly, God is committed to yet deal with the nation of Israel concerning their salvation and restoration.

Observation
If God were to repent on any of the above issues, He would be reversing His entire plan for Planet Earth and the coming Jewish kingdom. On these issues He will not repent:
- David, not Saul, will be king.
- Jerusalem will go into captivity.
- Christ will be an eternal priest.
- There will be a great tribulation.
- God will restore Israel.

God Did Not Repent
Jer. 20:16, *"...cities which the Lord overthrew, and repented not...."*

Zec. 8:14, "...to punish you...I repented not...."

In both cases, God's judgment came and was thorough, with no reprieve. He repented not.

God Does Not Repent

Num. 23:19; 1 Sam. 15:29.

Num. 23:19, "God is not a man, that he should lie; neither the son of man, that he should repent; hath he said, and shall be not do it? or hath he spoken, and shall he not make it good?"

Balak, the king of Moab, hires the heathen prophet Balaam to curse Israel. God meets the prophet and puts a blessing in his mouth instead. The king rebukes his hireling prophet, and arranges a supposedly more suitable location for curses. Again, God blesses Israel through the prophet. The prophet declares, *v. 20 - "Behold, I have received commandment to bless; and he hath blessed; and I cannot reverse it. God is not a man...that he should repent."* The king's rebukes are of no avail. The prophet is under Divine guidance, and God is not going to change in regard to Israel. God will not repent of blessing Israel.

Observation

For the prophet to stop blessing, and start cursing, would have been repentance on God's part. We see that repentance is a complete reversal on the issue in discussion.

Doctrinal Lesson

Some have quoted the prophet Balaam's words as a proof text, saying that God cannot repent. They tell us that the passage says that only men can repent; God can't. Notice: the passage does not say that God cannot repent: *"...hath he said, and shall he not do it?"* Concerning the issue at hand (the blessing of Israel), God is not as a man to go back on his word. God spoke the first time of a commitment to blessing. Balaam tells the king that a new position on the mountain is not going to move God to curse Israel. If this passage is dogma as to the attributes of God, declaring his inability to repent, then you have 38 other verses in contradiction. It is not that God is unable to repent in general, but that in this particular situation, where He has made a prior commitment, He cannot maintain His purpose and His integrity if He should repent concerning His covenant to bless Israel.

11

God Had Repented

Hos. 11:8; Jer. 15:6.

Jer. 15:6, "I am weary with repenting."

Many times God had repented of sending judgment. He is wearied from forestalling their just chastisement.

Observation

God has not only repented; He has done it so often He is wearied.

Conclusion to God's Repentance

God makes man on the earth, then repents and destroys him. He sets up Saul to be king and then repents and dethrones him. After leading the Israelites out of Egypt God decides to kill them all, but is persuaded to repent by the logic of Moses.

Many times God judges His people and sends evil, only to repent when He sees their suffering, is reminded of His covenant, or when they repent. God even repents of doing them good when they rebel.

There are, however, some covenant relationships or eternal programs of which under no circumstances will God repent.

These 39 uses of *repent* demonstrate that repentance is a total turn. It is not a desire or an intention to turn. It is not grief, sorrow, or remorse. It does not necessarily imply wrongdoing.

The verb *repent* is an action word. It is a doing. It is a turn from and to—from one thing, state, or act to the opposite. The important thing to see is that it is not mere sentiment. It is from north to south—from against to for.

With God, it was from creation to destruction, from life to death, from bondage to freedom, from freedom to bondage, from blessing to cursing, from cursing to blessing.

Man's Repentance Before God (66 uses)

Introduction

We have now come to the heart of the material. In examining the 66 uses of *repent* as they refer to man and his sin, or to man before God, we will see the dispensational differences in what God requires, from whom He requires it, and when He requires it. There is no question that in every dispensation men are commanded to repent regarding their sin or relationship to God. Yet the question we seek to answer is: "In this present dispensation, from what and to what must one repent in order to be saved?"

Man's Repentance Regarding Sin or God as Found in the Old Testament (6 uses)

1. *1 King 8:47* - v. *46-50*, *"If they sin against thee, ...and thou... carry them away captives...yet if they shall bethink themselves in the land...and repent and make supplication unto thee...saying, We have sinned, ...so return...with all their heart...and pray...then hear...And forgive...."*

"Bethink themselves" leads to repenting. As the Jew would consider the circumstances that led to his captivity, recognizing that it was his sin that caused God to send judgment, he would have a change of mind, heart, and direction. Thus, repentance begins with thinking about reality. The result was, they changed the condition that led to their captivity.

2. *Job. 42:6*, *"Wherefore I abhor myself, and repent in dust and ashes."*

God had declared Job to be *"a perfect and an upright man" (Job 1:8)*, yet Job repents. It was not from some act of disobedience or sin of the flesh that Job repents. Then from what or to what does he repent if he is judged by God to be *"perfect"*? In v. *42:3* Job says, *"...I uttered that I understand not; things too wonderful for me, which I knew not."* v. 5 - *"I have heard of thee by the hearing of the ear, but now mine eye seeth thee. Wherefore I abhor myself, and repent in dust and ashes."*

Job experienced what all believers will when we finally see God face-to-face—a realization that even at our very best, we are horrible. The words we spoke of Jesus while ministering here on earth were too wonderful to have fallen from our mortal lips. A renewed turn to behold Christ in all His glory is a repenting—a turning from our words and thoughts to Him alone.

3. *Ezek. 14:6,* *"Repent, and turn yourselves from your idols...."*
The issue that requires repentance is idolatry. In this situation repentance is nothing less than a complete turn from any act of idolatry. Sorrow or a willingness to turn is not enough.

4. *Ezek. 18:30.* Idolatry is again their problem. v. 15 *"Repent, and turn yourselves from all your transgressions...."*
An actual turn away from the transgression of idolatry is what God demanded.

5. *Jer. 8:6.* They are worshiping the, *v. 2 - "host of heaven."* God warns them and says, v. 6 - *"no man repented him of his wickedness."*
In all three of the passages above, repentance is simply turning from their idolatry back to the living God. Destroy your idols. Worship God.

6. *Jer. 31:19, v. 18,* *"...turn thou me, and I shall be turned; for thou art the Lord my God. Surely after that I was turned, I repented; and after that I was instructed, I smote upon my thigh; I was ashamed...."*
The Children of Israel were carried into captivity because of their idolatry, but God had made a covenant with their fathers, guaranteeing that they would inherit the land forever. The prophet anticipates a future date when God will lead His people Jacob out of all the nations where He has scattered them and bring them back into the land promised to their fathers. This and other passages predict that they will be brought back in unbelief. It is not until after they are restored to the land that they individually repent toward God and discover the faith of their fathers. This repentance is toward God, away from any unbelief or lack of faith. God repented them back to the land before they repented their hearts back to Him. Historically, their repentance back to the land is now a reality, and we await their repentance back to God.

John the Baptist Preaches Repentance (6 uses)

Matt. 3:2, "Repent ye: for the kingdom of heaven is at hand."
John was preparing them for a kingdom that never came; they crucified the King. God will yet *"restore again the kingdom to Israel" (Acts 1:6).* See also *Rom. 11:25-29.*

Matt. 3:11; Mark 1:4; Luke 3:3 will be discussed under **"Baptism and Repentance."**

Matt. 3:8; Luke 3:8 will be discussed under **"Fruits of Repentance."**

Observation
Repentance, under John, did not produce the new birth. John's repentance and baptism were not the same as that under the new covenant. *Acts 10:37; 18:25; 19:3-5.* John was part of the old covenant. *See Luke 7:28.*

The Nature of Repentance Under John the Baptist

Acts 19:4, "...saying unto the people, that they should believe on him which should come after him, that is, on Christ Jesus."
John was preparing the way for the Jewish Messiah to come to His people Israel. He required them to stop sinning *(Matt. 3:6, 8; Luke 3:11-14)*, and believe on Him "which should come after." The repentance he required was **away from** sin, **to** the Messiah.

Observation
John's repentance is different from God's repentance, old covenant repentance, and new covenant repentance.

Baptism and Repentance Mentioned Together (6 uses)

John preaches "baptism of repentance" in all six references.

Matt. 3:11; Mark 1:4; Luke 3:3; Acts 2:38; 13:24; 19:4.
John's baptism was an acceptance of *"the counsel of God against themselves" (Luke 7:30).*

God, in counsel with Himself, concluded that the Jews were in a most sinful state. John came to *"turn the hearts of the fathers to the children, and the disobedient to the wisdom of the just; to make ready a people prepared for the Lord" (Luke 1:17).*

Baptism was a public statement of one's need for the cleansing Messiah would bring. To not be baptized was to declare that one did not need to repent and did not need Messiah—a most self-incriminating omission.

Acts 19:4. The Apostle Paul clarifies John's position. *"John verily baptized with the baptism of repentance, saying unto the people, that they should believe on him which should come after him, that is, on Christ Jesus."*

John's converts were called on to *"bring forth therefore fruits worthy of repentance" (Luke 3:8)*, with belief in Christ to follow.

Observation

John's *"baptism of repentance"* was the return of the Jew to obey all the law in preparation for future faith in Messiah. No such precondition exists under this dispensation of faith and grace.

Peter Preaches Repentance and Baptism Together Only One Time

Acts 2:38, *"Then Peter said unto them, Repent, and be baptized every one of you in the name of Jesus Christ for the remission of sins, and ye shall receive the gift of the Holy Ghost."*

This is the only time after the institution of the Church that any apostle or new covenant preacher links repentance and baptism. This usage of *repent* throws significant light on the definition in the new covenant context. When Peter tells them to "repent," what is he telling them to do? With John, the issue was sin and a coming Messiah. But it is not so here. In the earlier verses of Acts 2, Peter goes into detail recounting the ministry of Christ. He calls to mind the miracles, quoting prophecy that Christ fulfilled in demonstration of His deity. He speaks to the very *"hands"* that detained, beat, and crucified Christ. He recounts Christ's resurrection. He then describes how Jesus is now seated at God's right hand, delivering on His promise of the Holy Ghost, *"which ye now see and hear."*

He concludes with: *"Therefore let all the house of Israel know assuredly, that God hath made the same Jesus, whom ye have crucified, both Lord and Christ. Now when they heard this they were pricked in their heart and said unto Peter and to the rest of the* apostles, *Men and brethren, what shall we do?" (Acts 2:36 37).*

Having seen their mistake in crucifying their own Messiah, they asked, *"what shall we do?"* How do we rectify this awful blunder? They obviously believed Peter's explanation, accepting that Christ was the Messiah.

Peter answers, *"Repent."* In regard to what you have done, change your mind, change your actions, change your heart. Turn **from** having rejected Messiah **to** accepting Him as Savior. Their repentance was not in regard to fornication, lying, love of money, complaining about low wages, or any personal sin. The repentance he demanded did not focus on the self, it focused on Jesus the Christ. Repent, turn in regard to Christ.

Jesus Preaches Repentance

Christ Himself is calling on men to turn. Since any repentance is a complete turnaround, what we particularly want to know is **from what** should we turn and **to what** should we turn in order to fulfill His command?

Matt. 4:17; 9:13; 11:20- 21; 12:41; 21:32; Mark 1:15; 2:17; Luke 5:32; 10:13; 11:32; 13:3, 5; 15:7, 10; 17:3- 4.

All of these references indicate the nature of the turn except *Matt. 4:17* and *Luke 13:3, 5.*

1. *Matt. 4:17, "...repent for the kingdom of heaven is at hand."*

2. *Luke 13:3, 5, "...except ye repent ye shall all likewise perish."*

Seven Events in the Preaching of Christ

The remainder of these verses (listed above) represent seven different events in the preaching of Christ, all of which indicate the same direction of turn—to faith in Christ.

1. *Matt. 21:32, v. 31, "For John came unto you in the way of righteousness, and ye **believed him not**; but the publicans and the harlots believed him; and ye, when ye had seen it, repented not afterward, **that ye might believe him.**"*

This statement follows a parable about a son who refused to go into the field to work, *"but afterward he repented, and went."* The Jews did not believe John's message concerning Who would come after, baptizing with the Holy Ghost. Jesus said, *"when ye had* *seen it, repented not **afterward**, that ye might believe him."* The Jews were not like the son in this parable. After they saw Christ, the reality of John's prediction, they still did not repent to believe.

Jesus was not, as John the Baptist, calling on the Jews to lay down their sin in preparation to believe. He was calling on them **to repent of not believing**. Their repentance was to be a turn **to** belief.

2. Matt. 12:41, v. 38, *"...Master, we would see a sign from thee... there shall no sign be given to it, but the sign of the prophet Jonas; the men of Nineveh... v. 41 - repented at the preaching of Jonas; and, behold, a greater than Jonas is here."*

See also Luke *11:32.*

John tells us, *"The Jews said unto him, What sign shewest thou them, that we may see, and believe thee?" (John 6:30).*

Again, the issue is believing. The Jews rejected Christ's person, holding out for just one more sign before believing.

3. Mark 1:15, *"...repent ye, and believe the gospel."* Now that Christ was present, the issue was "believe," turn ye and believe. Turn from your stubborn unbelief, demanding one more sign, and believe the gospel.

4. Matt. 11:20, 21; Luke 10:13. John's disciples came to Jesus with a doubt as to Jesus being the Christ. *"Art thou he that should come, or do we look for another?" (Matt. 11:3).* In verses 16-19, Jesus characterizes the unbelief of the Jews. In verses 20-24, He upbraids the cities that had rejected Him, *v. 20 - "because they repented not."* He finishes in verse 28 with, *"Come unto me, all ye that labour and are heavy laden, and I will give you rest."*

Again, the issue Christ raised was not acts of sin, but His own person. Would they believe and receive Christ? Even heathen Nineveh repented at the preaching of Jonah, and *"behold, a greater than Jonas is here."*

5. Mark 2:17; Matt. 9:13; Luke 5:32. Jesus went to a banquet at Levi's house. *Luke 5:30-32*—The *"Scribes and Pharisees murmured against his disciples, saying, Why do ye eat and drink with publicans and sinners? And Jesus answering said unto them, They that are whole need not a physician: buy they that are sick. I came not to call the righteous, but sinners to repentance."*

18

This demonstrates that Jesus is not indicating that the Pharisees are truly righteous while the ones He eats with are sinners. He tells them to *"learn what that meaneth"* if they would experience God's mercy instead of being sacrificed on the coals of Hell's altar. The *"publicans and sinners"* are receiving Him, and repenting. It is the Pharisees and Scribes that are rejecting, though in need of repentance. But they would have to learn that they were sinners before they could hear the call to Christ. A self-righteous man, as well as a man that thinks himself well, does not need Jesus the Physician.

Observation
The issue in this passage is the acceptance or rejection of Christ, not some act of sin or disobedience. The repentance the Pharisees needed was to repent of rejecting Christ.

6. *Luke 15:7 10, "Likewise, I say unto you there is joy in the presence of the angels of God over one sinner that repenteth."*

What is this sinner repenting **from** and **to** which causes rejoicing in heaven? What follows is the story of a son who leaves home and wastes his substance in riotous living. When he sees his need, he returns to the father broken and emptyhanded to be surprised by a full reception with all the honor and adornment of the righteous. The father causes all to gather to a great feast with rejoicing.

This is God's illustration of a sinner repenting. We don't see the sinner making himself worthy through putting away his sins or making vows of contrition. He comes as an embarrassing failure, with nothing to offer but a confession of sin and need. He is swept up into the father's arms to be clothed in the best robe and fed on the fatted calf. A repenting sinner is one who returns to his God and Father in absolute need.

Thus we again see that the object of (or direction of) repentance, as used in the new covenant salvation sense, is a turn to God. Separating one's self from sin is a result of coming **to** God, **not a precondition**.

7. *Luke 24:47.* After His resurrection, while making His first appearance to some of His disciples, Jesus opens their understanding of the Scriptures of the things concerning Himself. *"And that repentance and remission of sins should be preached in his name among all nations, beginning at Jerusalem."*

Again, the issue before us is not someone being told to stop sinning. As needful and appropriate as that is, having its place among those that are already saved, it is not an issue to be raised when preaching the gospel of the Lord Jesus Christ. **He** is the issue. Our failure is a well-attested and thoroughly demonstrated fact. The evangelist could not hope to call forth the least twitch of right-doing as a precondition for God to grant the new birth.

Observation

Since Jesus said to preach *"repentance and remission,"* not mentioning faith in the command, we therefore conclude that faith **is included** in new covenant (getting saved) repentance.

Conclusion to Jesus Preaches Repentance

With close examination, it is obvious that in all of Jesus' preaching on repentance, He never once comes close to suggesting that it has anything to do with the sinner dealing with his sins. When defined by the context, it is always **our relationship to Him** that is at issue. When the sinner is led to deal with his relationship to his sin as preparation for faith in Christ, he becomes committed to a process that can only lead to dead works, frustration, or self-righteousness. Our relationship to our sin is that of a leper to his disease. We do not put the disease away in order to be healed. We come to Christ and are healed before the symptoms ever disappear.

The Apostles Preach Repentance (6 uses)

Mark 6:12; Acts 2:38; 3:19; 8:22; 5:31; 2 Peter 3:9.

1. *Mark 6:12* *"And they went out, and preached that men should repent."*

While this verse does not define repentance, the following verses will.

2. *Acts 2:38* is dealt with under **"Repentance and Baptism."**

3. *Acts 3:19.* In v. 3:15, Peter begins, Ye *"Killed the Prince of life, whom God hath raised from the dead; whereof we are witnesses... through ignorance ye did it...But those things, which God before had shewed by the mouth of all the prophets, that Christ should suffer, he hath so fulfilled. Repent ye therefore, and be converted, that your sins may be blotted out...."*

Peter is telling them to repent (do a complete turnaround) in regard to the *"Prince of life"* whom they killed. Turn **from** your rejection **to** the blotting out of your sins. The issue then is the same today: "What will you do with Christ?" Not, "What will you do with your sin?" Christ has already dealt with your sin.

Observation

Since repentance is the only condition to the blotting out of sin, then faith must be an inherent part of new covenant repentance. Therefore, **repentance is not a separate act from faith.** They are one and the same objective reality. To "repent toward Christ" or "to believe on Christ" is the same function.

4. *Acts 8:22.* Here is a completely different usage of the word, in a different context altogether. *V. 13 - "Simon himself believed..." v. 18 "and when Simon saw that through laying on of the apostles' hands the Holy Ghost was given, he offered them money, Saying, give me also this power..." v. 20-22 - "But Peter said unto him, Thy money perish with thee, thou hast neither part nor lot in this matter; for thy heart is not right in the sight of God. Repent therefore of this thy wickedness, and pray God, if perhaps the thought of thine heart may be forgiven thee."*

Repentance is always a complete turnaround on the issue as defined by the context. In this passage Christ is not the direction of turn. The wicked thought of Simon's heart is that from which he must turn. In all cases where salvation is the subject, the sinner is told to repent regarding Christ. Here the subject is not salvation—rather, an offer of money to purchase apostolic powers. Of this, Simon must repent.

Observation

The broad application of the word is again manifest in this contrasting usage. Only the context defines the nature of the turn. Ceasing to do wickedness either in the heart or action is not extended to a nonbeliever as a condition of salvation.

5. *Acts 5:30 31,* *"...the God of our fathers raised up Jesus, whom ye slew and hanged on a tree. Him hath God exalted with his right hand to be a Prince and a Saviour, for to give repentance to Israel, and forgiveness of sins."*

Again, the context is having rejected and crucified the Messiah. God has demonstrated Jesus to be the Christ by resurrection and exaltation. Israel is to repent concerning Him.

6. 2 Peter 3:9, *"...there shall come in the last days scoffers, ...saying, where is the promise of his coming...The Lord is not slack concerning his promise, as some men count slackness; but is long-suffering to us-ward, not willing that any should perish, but that all should come to repentance."*

Again, the issue is Christ. The scoffers must come to repent concerning Him. The nature of the turn is **from** scoffing to **faith** in His person.

Conclusion to The Apostles Preach Repentance

Where repentance is preached in reference to the gospel (getting saved), the direction indicated is **always** to Christ, away from unbelief and rejection.

Keep in mind that these categories are all-inclusive. These verses are not selected. We record all that is in the Bible under the heading given.

Fruit of Repentance

With the understanding that repentance toward God will always result in causing the sinner to turn from his sin, many have confused the fruit with the root. They think that saving repentance is turning from sin. But that is getting the cart before the horse.

Fruit of Repentance Under John

Matt. 3:6 8; Luke 3:8 14; Acts 26:20; Titus 2:11-12.

Matt. 3:7, "But when he saw many of the Pharisees and Sadducees come to his baptism, he said unto them, O generation of vipers (sons of snakes), *who hath warned you to flee from the wrath to come? Bring forth therefore fruits meet for repentance...."*

Fruits that are *"meet"* are works that naturally accompany repentance. The nature of repentance was such that the fruit thereof would be consistent with the repentance. John warned them to demonstrate with their actions that they had indeed repented.

Luke 3:10, "And the people asked him, saying, what shall we do then? He answered and saith unto them, He that hath two coats, let him impart to him that hath none; and he that hath meat, let him do likewise. Then came also publicans to be baptized, and said unto him, Master, what shall we do? And he said unto them, Exact no more than that which is appointed you. And the soldiers likewise demanded of him, saying, And what shall we do? And he said unto them, Do violence to no man, neither accuse any falsely; and be content with your wages. "

In another instance, John rebuked King Herod for his adultery *(Matt. 14:3 4).*

John is requiring more than obedience to the law when he tells them to give up one of their coats, to share meat from their table and to be content with their wages. John requires the fruit of repentance **as a condition to** baptism. John's repentance is a turn from sin, not just a desire to turn, and not just a sorrow for sinning. They must stop sinning and act in a benevolent way to their fellowman. This is not the gospel of the Savior. **This is the law of preparation for the coming Messiah.** John is not preaching in the dispensation of the Church. He is still under the old covenant of the law. Imputed righteousness through faith in Christ awaits His coming death and resurrection.

Fruit of Repentance Under Paul

Acts 26:20, "But shewed...to the Gentiles, that they should repent and turn to God, and do works meet for repentance. "

Under John, the fruit of obedience was a precondition to baptism, whereas under Paul, works **followed** salvation.

Titus 2:11, 12, "For the grace of God that bringeth salvation hath appeared to all men, teaching us that, denying ungodliness and worldly lusts, we should live soberly, righteously, and godly, in this present world.... "

Observation

John's repentance was not the fruit of a relationship with Christ. It was a self-generated precondition to being baptized in preparation for the Messiah. It was not a subjective experience of remorse or personal commitment. **It was the actual act of ceasing to sin.** No such condition is ever laid on a sinner who would come to Christ.

Paul Preaches Repentance

There is a conspicuous absence of repentance preached in Paul's epistles—once in Romans and once in Hebrews. The second use of the word *repent* in Romans is a reference to God.

Romans, the book of how to be justified before God, speaks of faith and belief many times, but of man's repentance, only once. **Gal., Eph., Phil., Col., 1 & 2 Thes., 1 & 2 Tim., Titus, and Philem. never even use the word. Yet if repentance and faith are flip sides of the same act, then Paul is indeed preaching it when he speaks of faith.**

1. *Rom. 2:4,* *"Or despisest thou...his forbearance...not knowing that the goodness of God leadeth thee to repentance?"*

God's goodness is intended to impress upon the sinner the blessedness of being in fellowship with God and thereby lead one to repent toward God.

2. *Heb. 6:1,* *"...the foundation of repentance from dead works, and of faith toward God."*

This verse is a *"foundation"* in our study, a key to our understanding. The foundation of the Christian experience is clearly defined as repentance **from** (turn from) **dead works**, and of faith **toward** God. The two prepositions **"from"** and **"toward"** sum up repentance. As we have seen in the many uses and examples so far, any repentance is a complete turn. Any turn involves a turn from something **to** something. You can't turn **from** without turning **to**; you can't turn **to** without turning **from**. In this context, the object of the turn is defined explicitly as **from** dead works **to** faith in God.

3. *Heb. 6:4, 6,* *"For it is impossible for those who were once enlightened, and have tasted of the heavenly gift...If they shall fall away, to renew them again unto repentance; seeing they crucify to themselves the Son of God afresh, and put him to an open shame."*

Repentance has already been defined in verse one, but this sheds additional light. If new covenant repentance was turning from one's sin, it would always be possible, as long as one lived, to *"renew repentance."* But if repentance is turning *"toward God"* then one could not be renewed to this initial turn.

If the *"falling away"* is theoretical, so are the consequences; yet, the relationship remains in principle. If one fell away (turned away from his having turned to the crucified Christ), God could not renew him again to a turn from dead works to faith in God because he would subjectively experience the recrucifixion of Christ—something God says would put Christ to a renewed open shame.

4. *Rom. 11:29* is discussed under **"God and Repentance."**

5. *Acts 13:24* and ***Acts 19:4*** are discussed under **"Repentance and Baptism."**

6. *Heb. 12:17,* *"For ye know how that afterward, when he would have inherited the blessing, he was rejected: for he found no place of repentance, though he sought it carefully with tears."*

Esau sold his birthright for a bowl of soup. Later, when the blessing came due, he sought to repent (reverse his act), but was unable to effect a reversal.

Observation

This is a powerful example of the nature of repentance. It is **not a desire to turn** (Esau had that). It is **not sorrow** (Esau wept with sorrow). It is **not sincere, diligent seeking** (Esau sought diligently). It says, *"he found no place of repentance."* This shows that repentance is not something that occurs inside—not a sentiment. If he was full of care, seeking a *"place of repentance"* and couldn't find it, then repentance is not an inner feeling; it is the **act** of reversal. It could be a reversal of a belief, intention, or action, as the context defines.

7. *2 Cor. 7:9-11.* In 1 Corinthians, Paul rebukes the Church for many things, among which was their manner of dealing with a case of fornication by one of their members. In his second letter he says, *v. 8 - "For though I made you sorry with a letter, I do not repent, though I did repent;* (this "repent" is discussed under **"Man-to-Man Repentance"**) *for I perceive that the same epistle hath made you sorry, though it were but for a season. Now I rejoice, not that ye were made sorry, but that ye sorrowed to repentance: for ye were made sorry after a godly manner, that ye might receive damage by us in nothing. For godly sorrow worketh repentance to salvation not to be repented of: but the sorrow of the world* *worketh death...ye sorrowed after a godly sort, what carefulness it wrought in you, yea what clearing of yourselves...In all things ye have approved yourselves to be clear in this matter."*

This is a very distinct example of the variety of uses possible with the word *repent*. Paul's rebuke caused deep sorrow among the believers in Corinth. That sorrow moved them off their complacency, causing them to correct their error. They repented **from** the wrong way of dealing with the issue **to** the right way. They repented **from** their denominational divisions **to** a unity in Christ, **from** offending young brothers with their liberty **to** carefulness, **from** abuse of the Lord's table **to** sincere, reverent partaking, and **from** misuse of the gifts of the Spirit **to** edifying use.

Their repentance was not, as seen in the context of gospel preaching, a turn from dead works to God. That repentance cannot be renewed *(Heb. 6:6)*. Rather, they, being sorrowed by Paul's harsh letter of rebuke, went about to correct the errors he addressed.

Observation

Godly sorrow is just one among many things that can draw a **believer** to repentance. Obviously, an unbeliever cannot do anything godly—not even experience godly sorrow. Godly sorrow comes from grieving the Holy Spirit. The sorrow of a sinner is the *"sorrow of the world"* that *"worketh death."* The law of God *(Rom. 7:13)* *"works death"* in the unbeliever and, as a schoolmaster, brings him to Christ.

Let us not remove a verse from its context by giving it too sweeping of an application. If the emotion of sorrow were an essential part of "getting saved repentance," surely in all the messages to the unsaved, by Jesus, Paul, or the Apostles, it should be mentioned at least once. Yet in no place is sorrow mentioned in relationship to repentance except here, and that to believers only.

3. 2 Cor. 12:21, v.20, *"For I fear, lest when I come, I shall not find you such as I would...and that I shall bewail many which have sinned already, and have not repented of the uncleanness and fornication and lasciviousness which they have committed."*

This repentance that Paul is soliciting is to be performed by believers only, not sinners seeking to be saved. The Christians are to turn from—cease to do—the sins he names.

Observation

Under the new covenant, believers are called upon to repent of sins. There is not one example of an unsaved man commanded to repent of sins in order to be saved.

4. 2 Tim. 2:25, *"In meekness instructing those that oppose themselves: if God peradventure will give them repentance to the acknowledging of the truth...."*
The direction is clear. The turn desired is to acknowledge the truth—a turn from error to truth.

5. Acts 17:30, *"And the times of this ignorance God winked at; but now commandeth all men every where to repent...."*
Paul is in Athens on Mars' hill surrounded by hundreds of idols representing false gods. *Acts 17:29 - "...we ought not to think that the Godhead is like unto gold, or silver, or stone, graven by art and man's device."* He continues in verse 30 to tell them that up until now God had turned aside from judging such foolishness, but now He commands all men to repent (turn from idolatry to the living God).
Paul is not telling them to put away specific sins in order to be saved. He is telling them that they must stop seeing these images as gods, and turn to see Jesus, the resurrected one, as God.

Observation

Repentance in this context is a total turn to Jesus as God, and a turn away from any substitute god. The direction is still toward God. The object is not self dealing with sin; it is self coming to the true God.

6. Acts 26:20, *"...that they should repent and turn to God, and do works meet for repentance."*
Paul is standing before King Agrippa, giving his testimony of personal salvation as well as his call to apostleship and ministry. Verse 20 does not include the "steps to salvation;" it is a statement to Agrippa (his judge, who holds the power of life and death) of his ministry. He first tells his hearers to *"repent and turn to God,"* which we know from previously examined passages is the sum of what is required for remission of sins. He then exhorts them to do works that accompany (follow) true repentance. Jesus command-

ed his disciples to, *"teach them to observe all things whatsoever I have commanded you."*

Observation

When discussing the issue of "getting saved," works are never a part of repentance. This verse *(Acts 26:20)* separates works from the repentance. If works follow repentance, then works cannot be repentance.

The significant thing to see is that Paul never included *"works meet for repentance"* **as part of the gospel presentation.** Works were taught to believers afterward.

12. *Acts 20:21, "Testifying both to the Jews, and also to the Greeks, repentance toward God, and faith toward our Lord Jesus Christ."*

This verse says it most clearly. Repentance is toward God. Repentance is faith toward Christ. It is as the marriage vow: "Forsaking all others, I take Him."

Conclusion to Paul Preaches Repentance

Paul uses the word *repent* five different ways:
- God and repentance.
- Man-to-man repentance.
- John's baptism of repentance.
- Repentance from dead works toward God for salvation.
- The Christian repenting of individual acts of sin.

The varied use is obvious in Paul's letters, while he maintains very strict boundaries of distinction. To ignore the dispensational character of repentance can lead, as it has with many, to the preaching of a false gospel.

The Book of Revelation and Repentance

The Church is Commanded to Repent (6 uses)

1. *Rev. 2:5, v. 4,* *"...thou has left thy first love. Remember therefore from whence thou art fallen, and repent, and do the first works...."*

The Church at Ephesus was told to repent back to their first love. Remembering the joys of their first love, they should be motivated to desire it and turn back to it.

2. *Rev. 2:16, v. 15,* *"So hast thou also them that hold the doctrine of the Nicolaitans, which thing I hate. Repent; or else I will come unto thee quickly..."*

The Church had already degenerated into a structural class system with ministers assuming a superior role. God said that He hated this doctrine and commanded the Church to repent from it. "Discard this false doctrine, or I will come in judgment."

3. *Rev. 2:22, v. 20,* *"...thou sufferest that woman Jezebel...to teach and to seduce my servants to commit fornication, and to eat things sacrificed unto idols. Behold, I will cast her into a bed, and them that commit adultery with her into great tribulation, except they repent of their deeds."*

Here, the Church is commanded to repent of specified deeds (sinful deeds). This emanated from an association with a woman teacher. From this, the Church should repent.

4. *Rev. 3:3, v. 2,* *"...For I have not found thy works perfect before God. Remember therefore how thou hast received and heard, and hold fast, and repent."*

The Church is commanded to repent of imperfect works. He said the Church was *"dead."* Again, to *"remember"* was to provoke them to repent. Remember how it was and turn back.

5. *Rev. 3:19, v. 15,* *"...thou art neither cold nor hot; v. 19 ...be zealous therefore, and repent."*

The Church of the first century had degenerated to a place similar to that of the Church today. Lukewarmness was the rule. "Repent" was God's command. They had been hot and were now lukewarm. They needed to repent back to being hot. The cure was to let Jesus back into His Church. *"...open the door, I will come in to him..."*

Observation

The Church is commanded to repent from:
- Leaving their first love.
- The Doctrine of the Nicolaitans.
- The teacher Jezebel, and evil deeds (sin).
- Imperfect works.
- Lukewarmness.

Only believers possessed by the Spirit of God are in a position to repent from sin. Thus, God expects all that name the name of Christ to depart from iniquity. This demonstrates a variation of the usage of the word as compared to its use in gospel preaching.

The Heathen Do Not Repent in the Book of Revelation (6 uses)

Rev. 2:21 (2 uses); *Rev. 9:20-21; 16:9, 11.*

1. & 2. Rev. 2:21, *"And I gave her space to repent of her fornication; and she repented not."*

The "Mother of Harlots" still plies her trade of spiritual adultery, feeding the faithless on "holy wafers" offered to idols. She still will not have repented in *Rev. 17:18* when they *"burn her with fire."*

3. Rev. 9:20, *"And the rest of the men which were not killed by these plagues yet repented not of the works of their hands, that they should not worship devils and idols...."*

During the Great Tribulation God will demonstrate that the human heart is intent on evil by giving men a foretaste of Hell with "space to repent." God is vindicated as they, one by one, shake their fists in His face in stubborn rebellion.

4. Rev. 9:21, *"Neither repented they of their murders, nor of their sorceries, nor of their fornication, nor of their thefts."*

As in Nineveh, repentance from these fleshly sins would bring a stay of execution, a lifting of God's evil judgments, but not personal redemption. The day of regeneration passed with the rapture of the saints.

5. Rev. 16:9, *"And men were scorched with great heat, and blasphemed the name of God, which hath power over these plagues; and they repented not to give him glory."*

The direction of repentance that God expected was to bring glory to his Name rather than blasphemy.

6. Rev. 16:11, *"...And blasphemed the God of heaven because of their pains and their sores, and repented not of their deeds."*

God is pouring out the worst of His judgments, supernaturally keeping men alive so they cannot escape through the door of death. Yet, with an impending threat of eternal damnation, they still will not repent of their deeds or give God glory.

Observation

In these six uses, the repentance that the sinner failed to do was a failure to turn from sin, whereas when the Apostles preached repentance it was a turn to God. The fact that not one soul out of millions repents of sin is demonstration that apart from the grace of God none would repent. How could something be a precondition to the new birth if men cannot do it? (Cannot because they will not.)

Repent and Believe/Faith

It is interesting to note that out of the 66 uses of *repent* and the hundreds of uses of *faith* or *believe*, they are linked together only three times.

1. Mark 1:15, v. 14, *"Jesus came...preaching the gospel of the kingdom of God, And saying, the time is fulfilled, and the kingdom of God is at hand: repent ye, and believe the gospel."*

This is very different from what John the Baptist preached. John **never preached faith** as part of his repentance. Paul tells us in Acts 19:4 that John said unto the people, *"that they should believe on him which should come after him, that is, on Christ Jesus."* John was preparing them **to believe** on Christ when He would come.

Christ's message was *"repent ye, and believe the gospel."* But Mark does not define the nature of this repentance. Was it the same repentance that John preached? **From** what and **to** what is one to turn in believing the gospel?

2. Acts 20:21, *"Testifying both to the Jews, and also to the Greeks, repentance toward God and faith toward our Lord Jesus Christ."*

Here is a passage defining the direction of the turn – *"repentance toward God."*

3. Heb. 6:1, *"...the foundation of repentance from dead works, and of faith toward God."*

Again we have the direction of turn defined. **Turn away from dead works to God.**

What are *"dead works"*? Dead works are any effort of man to achieve favor with God through right doing. A man who is *"dead in trespasses and sins"* can only produce *"dead works."* Those who hope that through obedience and surrender they will gain salvation are engaging in dead works as are those who attempt to "repent of their sins" in order to prepare themselves to believe.

To *"repent from dead works"* is to turn **from** all human effort **to** the God of redemption. It is even a turn from your turning. It is not seeing merit even in your emptiness. It is seeing that there is no merit in not seeing merit. It is a turn to God as the only hope without giving consideration to the turn.

Observation

Repentance is always a total turn from something to something. Only the context defines the object of the turn. God defines new covenant, salvation repentance as a **turn away from dead works to the living God.**

Repentance Preached to the Unsaved in This Dispensation

Every reference to the preaching of repentance in this dispensation is distinguished by its lack of confronting the sinner with any expectation that he should cease sinning as a condition for acceptance. Where the context offers any suggestion as to the nature of repentance, it is always synonymous with faith and has Christ as its focus. All of these verses have been discussed under **"The Apostles Preach Repentance"** and **"Paul Preaches Repentance."**

Acts 2:38; 3:19; 5:31; 11:18; 17:30; 20:21; 26:20; Rom. 2:4; 2 Tim. 2:25; Heb. 6:1.

There is also Christ's commission for this dispensation: *Luke 24:47.*

Observation

There is absolutely no scriptural basis for telling a sinner to "repent of his sins" in order to be saved. To do so is to preach *"another gospel."* If you want to preach repentance from sin to sinners, you will have to wait until the latter part of the tribulation. The results, however, have already been tallied *(Rev. 9:20, 21; 16:9, 11).*

There is a need in this dispensation for the preaching of repentance from sin to **believers**. The Church (those who are the genuinely saved) needs to repent from sins. *The Church has the power* to repent from sins, while the unsaved are incapable of it until they receive the Holy Spirit's power.

We have seven new covenant examples of the Church or its members called upon to repent of specific sins: *Acts 8:22; Rev. 2:5, 16, 22; 3:3, 19; 2 Cor. 12:21.*

Remember, a believer cannot be renewed again to the repentance that saves *(Heb. 6:6)*; it's a one time repentance to God, while repentance from sin is a daily occurrence for the Spirit-filled believer.

Personal Evangelism in the Book of Acts

Acts 8:12, 37; 9:1 22; 10:43; 11:17; 13:38, 48; 14:1; 15:9; 16:14, 31, 34; 17:3 4, 30, 34; 18:8; 19:5, 18; 28:23, 24.

In *Acts*, our history book of the early Church, there are 15 accounts of personal evangelism described. Not once is a sinner told to (nor does it say he did) repent in reference to his sins. Paul uses the word *repent* one time on Mars hill. It is from idolatry to the living God that they are to repent.

Note: *Acts 10:43* and *Acts 11:17*. Peter preached to the Gentiles and they were saved, and this without mentioning repentance. Yet when he testifies of it, the Church responded with, *"Then hath God also to the Gentiles granted repentance unto life" (Acts 11:18).* "Believe" was Peter's message (Acts 10:43). Believe is what they did *(Acts 11:17).* Yet the Church, hearing that they had believed, called it *"repentance unto life."* Therefore, following the Apostle's example, we are to tell the sinner to believe. God gives the repentance—the turn of the heart to God.

The verses listed above abound with faith and belief as the condition or the stated response of the sinner being saved. "Repent" is conspicuously absent, although in every case, doubtlessly, repentance toward God and faith toward Christ was occurring as the sinner believed.

On two occasions, when Paul was testifying of his ministry, he used *repent* to describe his message:

Acts 20:21, "...repentance toward God...."

Acts 26:20, "...repent and turn to God...."

In both cases it is defined as *"toward God."* Paul never laid on the sinner the responsibility of dealing with his sins. He was led to deal with the Savior by faith.

Three times, early in the book of Acts, the Jews who rejected and crucified Christ were challenged to repent concerning Him. *(Acts 2:38; 3:19; 5:3)*

Miscellaneous Passages and Points Examined

Matt. 27:3 - "Then Judas, which had betrayed him, when he saw that he was condemned, repented himself, and brought again the thirty pieces of silver to the chief priests and elders, Saying, I have sinned in that I have betrayed the innocent blood...And he cast down the pieces of silver in the temple, and departed, and went and hanged himself."

Judas did not repent toward God. He *"repented himself."* His turn was a self-generated sorrow for the consequences of his wrongdoing. He tried to undo his sinful deed. He tried to make it right. In short, **Judas repented of his sin**. Yet, like Esau *(Heb. 12:17), "He found no place of repentance, though he sought it carefully with tears."* This demonstrates the futility of man's puny effort in dealing with his own sin. <u>Judas was attempting to do the very thing that many evangelists demand of those who would be saved.</u> Judas didn't lack zeal or commitment in his repentance; he lacked a Savior. His focus was wrong. **He was dealing with his sin rather than dealing with the Savior.** If he had gone to Christ (repented toward God) he would have found forgiveness.

John Never Uses the Word *Repent* in His Gospel

John uses the word *believe* (in any of its forms) 98 times. Many times John tells us how to have life through Jesus Christ. Yet, he never found it necessary to tell his readers to repent. If *repent*, in the new covenant context, is an act separate from belief, then John's gospel is incomplete.

We cannot but assume that new covenant belief includes repentance. Repentance and belief (in the new-birth context) are the same reality. Why two words? Why are the words *repent and believe* used together only one time in the Scripture? *(Mark 1:15)* The answer as to why there are two words for the same experience becomes obvious when we examine the circumstances in which one word is chosen over the other. Repent is stating the negative side of a turn. Believe (or faith) is stating the positive side—two sides of the same coin—one reality. This is not necessarily so when repent is used in another context. Our concern is to define *repent* when used as the condition for the new birth.

The word "repent" is appropriate when the one addressed is clinging to a false foundation that is in competition with God. "Believe" is appropriate when the sinner has no foundation or any other hope. To the idolaters on Mars hill, Paul says, *"repent."* To the Philippian jailer he says, *"believe."*

One who rejects true faith for a false system of belief must repent of the false foundation. Whereas the one hopelessly bound in unbelief, with no competing religious foundation, needs only to believe on the Lord Jesus Christ. To oversimplify it: "Repent" is believing away from a false belief. "Faith" is believing toward God.

John's gospel is a positive gospel. He assumes that when Christ is lifted up He will draw all men unto Himself. In John's gospel *"he that believeth not"* **is** the unrepentant; *"He that believeth"* **is** the repentant.

Repent of Your Sins?

It may be shocking to you to discover that the most often spoken and printed phrase in the Christian vocabulary, "repent of sin," does not appear in the Scripture. The closest thing to it is the statement of Peter to Simon, who seeks to buy the powers of apostleship. Peter tells him to, *"Repent therefore of this thy wickedness" (Acts 8:22).* Simon is a professing believer, though it is doubtful that he was saved. Peter is not giving Simon the gospel—the road to salvation. He is telling him that he should repent of thinking he can buy the powers of apostleship with money. Not once in Scripture is the condition of sin, or the state of being a sinner, referred to as something to "repent of." This is a heresy created by Satan himself to put a stumbling block between the sinner and Christ.

Also, in the book of Revelation, we are told that the heathen will not repent of idolatry, fornication, witchcraft, deeds, etc. Notice that these are all individual acts of sin from which they are to turn. They were not promised salvation if they repented. Though it was implied that the terrible tribulation judgments would have been lifted if they had repented. **If a sinner must "repent of sin" in order to be saved, as many preachers declare, then why does neither the term nor the concept ever appear in Scripture?**

How could a teaching so far removed from the truth and conspicuously absent from Scripture gain such acceptance in the Church? There are several possibilities:

• It is such a reasonable and logical teaching. We are told that, "After all, it is our sin that separates us from God. God wants us to stop sinning. Get rid of the sin and everything will be all right." But conservative theology recognizes man's inability to rise above sin. Thus repentance is reduced to a mere "willingness" to stop sinning. The sinner is then told that if he will repent of wanting to sin, God will empower him to stop, which then clears the way for salvation. Theoretically, this "repent of sin to be saved" theology is true according to natural revelation. That is, plain reason tells us that if a man stopped sinning he would be a better person. He deserves some consideration from God. He is due a show of grace for past sins since he is not going to continue in sin. Practically, repenting of sin in order to be saved is an absurdity that must either redefine sin or redefine repentance. Historically, no man has ever completely repented of sin as preparation for God. If one could do so, the cross would not be necessary. The cross is where God executes sinners with their sin and raises them to life anew.

God separates the sinner from his sin only after he is born again. It is a process defined in the Epistles that takes a lifetime of repenting of sins and reckoning one's self dead to sin. To make it a precondition to salvation is to *"...bind heavy burdens and grevious to be borne, and lay them on men's shoulders; but they themselves will not move them with one of their fingers" (Matt. 23:4).*

No evangelist that demands the sinner "repent of his sin" in order to be saved has yet repented of all his. Ask his wife.

• Another possible cause of the proliferation and entrenchment of error concerning repentance is the zeal of would-be theologians attempting to purge and protect the ranks of professing Christians.

The presence of large numbers of tares in the wheat causes us to want to define salvation in such a way as to erode the confidence of false professors. We see them boasting of "God's sovereign grace," while they feast the flesh on the world's fare. An evangelist throws open the gate of salvation and we watch with consternation as Judases pour in to dilute the integrity of the ranks. The title "easy believism" has been attached to those who do not shake down the sinner at the door.

In an attempt to weed out the halfhearted, "guardians of the faith" have created an "entrance exam"—a passing score being: "sufficient fruits of repentance." Those who have become comfortable in the grace of God have raised the standard for entrance to the point that, if they took their own test, they themselves would fail.

We have no right to tamper with God's standard of admission. **Only by reducing repentance to mere sentiment can it be made into a condition for man to meet.** When properly understood, the standard is far beyond the sinner's reach, far too high for any to qualify. Only the cross purges the sinner and separates him from his sin.

• Yet another cause of the sustained error concerning repentance is the failure to "rightly divide the Word of Truth." When one fails to view repentance dispensationally, the resulting confusion is enormous. Don't say you don't believe in dispensations if you are not offering animal sacrifices and stoning your disobedient children. Christ placed John the Baptist in a different dispensation. God has clearly defined repentance for this dispensation. Don't go to another dispensation to build your doctrine.

• Perhaps the one thing that has contributed most to the erroneous ideas on repentance is **personal experience**. For many of you the salvation experience was the climax of a long weary struggle in which the Holy Spirit overpowered your consciences. The things of this world, along with personal lusts, were discarded for the life-saving promises. When you heard the call of the Holy Spirit, the things most precious, the things you thought you could never give up, lost their luster and were thoughtlessly cast aside. You came empty-handed, yet with no thought as to what you had forsaken or left behind. You embraced Christ as your all-in-all. It was a marriage made in heaven. Years later, looking back on that time of "coming under conviction" and attempting to define the path that others must follow, it seems that, surely, you "repented of your sins" in order to be saved. Did not you forsake all? The answer is, NO! you did not. Your understanding of spiritual reality was so limited that if you could have judged then as you judge now you would have crawled into a hole for shame, never daring approach God on the basis of repenting of anything. Don't lay burdens on men that you didn't bear. Don't cause men to approach God in self-righteousness. Don't rob God of the glory of saving sinners. **You cannot translate your subjective experience into a road map that others must follow.**

Get your definitions from the Bible, not from your experience. Don't preach your experience. That is tantamount to preaching yourself. Preach Christ and let the Word Itself bear fruit as it did in you. Resign your position as vice-chairman of the entrance committee. God has no official Tare Pullers. Quit trying to be one.

• Another reason error has been admitted into our repentance theology is on philosophical grounds. The great questions of existence and destinies are fertile ground for a discussion of repentance. Why do some ultimately perish while others are saved? Why me, Lord? Why am I saved when others are lost? How is God vindicated in saving some? Why does He not save all? What does God see in one man but not in another?

We mentally create a moral dilemma for God and then absolve Him of guilt by ascribing worthiness to those He saves and lack of merit to the damned. Ultimately, our carnal conclusion is: "God helps those who help themselves by repenting of their sins. Those who don't repent of their sins are damned."

Our need to allow the Scripture to be our sole guide is evident when we try to be philosophers. God does not need to be vindicated in His eternal decrees (whatever that may be), nor do we need to justify His discretion in whom He saves or doesn't. Just "preach the Word."

This popular concept of repentance is well supported by human reason, being based on natural principles of retribution, judgment, and mercy. By natural law, one could demonstrate the reasonableness of the Sadducees' position, *"which say that there is no resurrection" (Matt. 22:23).* Everyone knows by experience that "when you're dead, you're dead." Yet when Divine revelation becomes a factor, experience and natural laws are no longer significant. The present dispensation with its repentance for salvation is not the same as that of Moses' and John the Baptist's dispensation.

The entrance of Jesus Christ as a substitutionary offering to God is foreign to our general principles. His vicarious righteousness and atonement has injected an element beyond the bounds of mortal relationships and legal proceedings.

This gospel is not the message of God assisting the sinner to reach heaven's standards. It is the message of God having, as a fact of history, already met His own demands in the person of His Son. This is *"foolishness to the world,"* and is very seldom understood. God's substitution allows Him to *"justify the ungodly."* God is not vindicated by the reformed condition of the sinner. **There is no justification for God saving any sinner, except in the history of Jesus Christ.** Only the historical act of the cross of Christ allows God to be *"just and the justifier of them which believe in Jesus."*

Is salvation based on God assisting us to obey, or is it Christ's obedience on our behalf? Is it God's work **in us**, or is it Christ's work **for us**? Is our salvation based on God giving us a new life, or Christ giving His life in our place?

One of these answers is reasonable and understandable to the carnal mind. In fact, all religions would together give assent to one of the above. The other answer is not natural. It is a miracle of incarnation, substitution, sacrifice, death, and resurrection. One is an assisted, earned degree. The other is a free gift with but one act of obedience: **"believe."**

A theology which makes man's repentance (howbeit a gift of God) the ground of redemption is a *"doctrine of men"* shared by all religions. It is a teaching of purely human, or Satanic, origin. Though it is the "historical position," it is a Christless theology. The "repent of your sins in order to be saved" theology has no es-sential need of a suffering Savior. It finds sufficient justification for saving the sinner within the response of the sinner himself. May God grant us *"repentance to the acknowledging of the truth, that in all things he might have the preeminence."*

Most fundamentalists falsely view repentance as a prepara-tory work that God does in the individual, a work that sets him apart for salvation. It is supposed that it is this change **in** the sin-ner that constitutes the basis of God saving him. This "state of repentance," we are told, changes his heart, the set of his mind, the placement of his affections, and guarantees that works will follow.

Repentance is falsely viewed as a wrestling with the angel of conviction, culminating in the loss of pride, self-strength, and love of sin. It results in a total yielding of the "self-nature" to be controlled by God. It is making Jesus "Lord of all." It is seen as a "giving over; a giving up; a dying; a laying it all down to take up the cross." It is "dying to self so Christ can sit on the throne of the heart." In short, it is "getting right with God."

This "rightness," coming into the sinner before he is saved, supposedly forms a basis for God to save him. To avoid the indict-ment of creating works salvation, the subjectivists hastily explain that, "It is God's grace working in the sinner." We ask, "God's grace working in the sinner doing what?" Working in one of the Devil's children creating a clean heart and a right spirit before the Holy Spirit indwells him? Does God save a sinner because he

has already been separated from his sin, or in order **to** separate him from his sin? Those who do not find the atonement alone to be sufficient ground for God saving the ungodly use the sinner's repentance from sin (aided by God as that may be) to justify God's discrimination in saving one sinner and not another.

This "repentance state" into which God would bring the sinner would, to the average sense of common justice, constitute a legitimate ground for a discharge of Divine mercy. When a condemned criminal accepts all blame, humbly offering restitution, even the most demanding legalist is moved to display mercy. We would view it as another kind of immorality for the righteous not to forgive when repentance is so sincerely displayed. The contrition of the condemned draws out an emotion that makes us think that it is obligatory for God to forgive the repentant. According to subjective sentiment, his brokeness seemingly obligates the court of heaven to judge with mercy. Likewise, a common sense of justice leaves us feeling that those who are impenitent and unbroken in no way deserve mercy. They bear the burden of their own condemnation.

The courts and judgments of men are moved by subjective considerations. Society is built on common assent to the unspoken rules of fair play (judgment tempered with deserving mercy). Undeserved mercy is viewed as lawlessness, weakness, or corruption. We automatically transfer these principles to God as rules for his behavior. **There must be in the accused a response that justifies any court's display of mercy.**

What it comes down to is this: We look into the heart of the guilty to decide of what punishment or mercy he is worthy. We feel that the judge's judgments **must be justified in the accused himself.** But if popular sentiment were correct there would be no necessity for vicariousness in the imputation of righteousness. If one were forgiven in response to his repentance from sin, the cause of justification would be in the change made in the supposedly former sinner, not in the provision of a gift of vicarious righteousness and atonement. <u>His repentance would be his atonement.</u> His savior would be his conscience that has moved him to restitution. **He would not be moved to Christ, rather, to obedience.** Christ would not be substituting Himself for one who needed something he didn't have; the sinner would be providing repentance in substitution for his former life of sin.

Conclusion

There is a human propensity, based on the "the pride of life," to pay for everything we receive. Indebtedness is a humbling state. Long before men will bow in surrender to God, they will stand to make an offering, or they will surrender and then count the sacrifice and humility of it a worthy and meritorious plea for mercy.

Preachers aid this religious drive by providing a doctrinal context in which the flesh can justify its need to make a contribution to its own redemption. It is the religion of repentance itself that often prevents a man from the utter despair that would lead to true repentance. Many sinners have traded in their active rebellion or passive indifference for active surrender. Surrender, which looks around for approval, is a con man's game. Men fall short of trusting God by trusting their own trust. Men fall short of repenting to God by repenting from their sins.

The whole work of the law is to bring men to a place of despair and defeat. Utter hopelessness in our own strength gives way to utter trust in Christ. A sinner who offers to God his repentance is far from defeated. A sinner who offers to God his defeat is far from trusting God.

The mark of true repentance and faith is that one involuntarily, unconsciously ceases to focus on himself and becomes enraptured with the wonder of God's Lamb. A truly repentant man will **never** (not now, nor in the future) make reference to his own condition as a contributing factor to his salvation. Those who lower themselves for salvation are rejected as are those who exalt themselves. It is as dangerous to focus on your lack of merit as it is to promote your own works.

To lead a sinner to think upon, consider, or in any way alter "the self" in preparation for salvation is to lead him into a morass of works. The repentance that improves a man's standing before God is an inclining to self-righteousness.

If while *"we were yet without strength, in due time Christ died for the ungodly"* (Rom. 5:6), then we can come as **we are**. We already qualify. Adam did all that was necessary to qualify us for Christ. It took 4000 years of instruction and law to bring the human race to appreciate its need. The high calling of the law, filled in the teachings of Christ, has totally divested us of hope.

Preachers, you fall into the Devil's plan, as his last best wedge between the sinner and Christ, when you motivate sinners to the activity of repenting of their sins in order to be saved. Preach the law as God's unalterable, eternal, and reasonable demand on all flesh. Preach the holy character of God through Biblical examples. Allow the sinner to wilt in despair before his Maker. Only a minister who holds in suspense the mystery of the gospel of grace can, with all its fury, release the relentless law of God on a feeble sinner.

When the Holy Spirit has done His work through the Word of law, then and only then can you offer the fountain of life to a thirsty soul. At this point, to direct the sinner to repent of his sins would be the gravest of errors. Let him see Jesus as God's complete answer to his complete need. **The sinner's transfer of all hope and confidence to the trust of Jesus alone is the heart and soul of salvation repentance.** Repentance and faith are one and the same act-less act. **It is the antitheses of doing.** Even the act of surrender is the fruit of repentance and faith. If people everywhere are to be saved, then those who preach must preach the pure gospel of Christ until men and women repent of their self-generated repentance and simply **believe God**.

For other Bible study materials taught by Michael Pearl contact:
No Greater Joy, 1000 Pearl Road, Pleasantville, TN 37033
1-866-292-9936
or visit our online store at www.NoGreaterJoy.org
When ordering, ask for our free magazine.

Bible Study Audio:
Matthew
John
Romans
(Go to our website to download
Mike's entire teaching on the
book of Romans in MP3 and
other messages FREE!)
1 Corinthians
Ephesians
Colossians
Galatians
Hebrews
Mark
Am I Saved?
Balaam & His Ass
Body, Soul, & Spirit
By Divine Design
Chronological Prophecies
Generational Sins
God's Eternal Program
God Hates Sinners
Repentance
Righteousness
Sabbath Rest
Sanctification
Security of the Believer
Sinful Nature
Sin No More
Sons of God and Giants
When Forgiveness is Sin

Bible Study Books:
Romans Chapter 1-8
  Commentary
Revelation Poster And Handbook
Eight Kingdoms
Good and Evil
1 John 1:9 the Protestant
  Confessional
Baptism in Jesus' Name
In Defense of Biblical
  Chastisement
Justification and the book of James
Pornography - Road to Hell
To Betroth or not to Betroth
By Divine Design